About This Book

WELCOME TO THE fascinating world of home music-making.
This course will help you get the best out of your electronic keyboard – the most versatile instrument yet invented.

By the end of Book 1 you will be:

- **Reading Music**
- **Playing popular melodies** in many different styles
- **Easily adding complete accompaniments** consisting of bass notes, chords and drums to all your songs.

Although written primarily as a 'teach yourself' method, *The Complete Keyboard Player* books have been taken up eagerly by teachers (individual and classroom) all over the world.

This latest edition has been brought completely up to date, reflecting the changes and improvements in keyboards over the years, and introducing some new hit songs, while retaining many of the old favourites.

Good luck!

Kenneth Baker

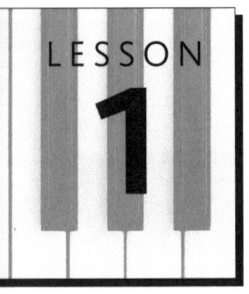

Your Keyboard

ALTHOUGH MODERN KEYBOARDS vary from make to make and model to model, they all have the same basic features:

Power (mains)
Turns the keyboard on or off. Most keyboards can run on batteries or from the mains, using a suitable transformer, which is usually supplied with your keyboard.

Master Volume
This controls the overall 'loudness' of the instrument. It is either in the form of a slider, button or knob, which can be set anywhere from minimum to maximum.

Auto-accompaniment
This feature adds an automatic accompaniment to your melody, which you can use in various different ways.

Tempo (Speed)
This controls the speed of the accompaniment rhythm. Can be set anywhere from minimum to maximum, or may display an exact tempo, e.g. ♩=112. The number displayed is the number of beats per minute, and varies between about 45 to about 220.

Synchro-start
This button activates the auto-accompaniment and synchronises it to when you start playing.

Rhythm or Style
This feature adds a drum rhythm to your melody. You can choose between a number of different styles, e.g. rock, pop, latin, swing etc.

Voices or Solo Sounds
These might be grouped in different 'types' of voice, e.g. strings, woodwind, or they may be grouped by instrument, depending on how many different voices your particular keyboard offers. They add colour and interest to your melodies.

Information Screen
Most modern keyboards incorporate a digital screen which provides information about which settings you are using, e.g: which voice and rhythm you have selected, and whether you are using auto-accompaniment.

See your owner's manual for specific details.

Sitting At Your Keyboard

SET UP YOUR keyboard on its own stand or on a table of medium height.

Sit facing the centre of the instrument and adjust your seat so that your arms are level with the keyboard, or sloping down slightly towards it.

Support your hands from the wrists. Imagine that you are holding a rather fragile ball and curve your fingers lightly around it.

With the tips of your fingers, cover any five adjacent white notes in each hand.

This is your normal, most relaxed playing position. After all fingering and hand changes during a piece, you should return to this position.

Finger Numbers

Your fingers are numbered OUTWARDS from the thumbs, like this:

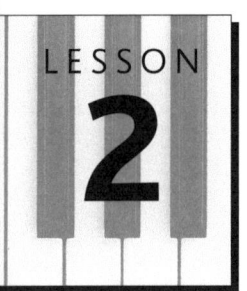

Warm Up

SWITCH ON YOUR KEYBOARD and turn up the **master volume**, and any subsidiary volume controls you may have, to about halfway.
Check that your **auto-accompaniment** control is switched to normal (or off):

Select a voice, say **piano**:

The **voices** (solo sounds) on your keyboard might be divided into general categories, such as **keyboards**, **woodwind**, **brass**, **strings**, and so on (a bit like an orchestra). In the example above, where we are aiming to set up a **piano**, go into **keyboards**, press **01** on the number pad (01 is an almost universal number set up for basic piano sound) and the piano sound will appear on the screen.

Run your finger along the keys from left to right and note the piano sounds progressing from Low to High. Now run your finger along the keys in the opposite direction and note the progression from High to Low.

Set up a **violin** sound for yourself. Go to **voices**, then **strings**. Find the number for violin and select it.
Play a few single notes at random in the middle to upper range of your keyboard and listen to the sound of the violin.

Now Let's Play Some Rhythm

THERE WILL BE MANY different rhythm patterns (sometimes called **styles**) available on your keyboard. Like voices, rhythms will probably be subdivided into **categories**. Typical rhythm categories are **rock**, **pop**, **ballroom** and **latin**:

In your **rock** category, select one of the rock variations, for example **rock pop** and press **start**. Listen to this rhythm pattern for a few moments, then try speeding it up or slowing it down using your **tempo** control:

Try other rock variations, or totally different rhythms, such as **quickstep** (probably in the **ballroom** category) or **bossa nova** (probably in the **latin** category).

Now, instead of the **start** button, select **synchro**, or **synchro-start**.
Play any note in the lower register (the lower half of the keyboard) and the rhythm section will start automatically.
Press **synchro** again and the rhythm will stop.

We shall be using this useful feature in a song soon.

Black And White Notes

YOUR KEYBOARD HAS a number of black and white keys*. The black keys are divided into groups of twos and threes, and these same groups repeat all along the keyboard:

You need these black key groups in order to locate the white notes and find your way around.

Your First White Note: C

C is a very commonly used white note. The C's lie directly to the left of each group of two black notes:

The Other Six White Notes

The musical alphabet runs from A to G, then repeats itself over and over again.
In other words, there are only seven different white notes to learn:

* The exact number of keys varies from model to model.

8

Your Second White Note: G

The G notes lie here, within each group of three black notes:

Splitting The Keyboard

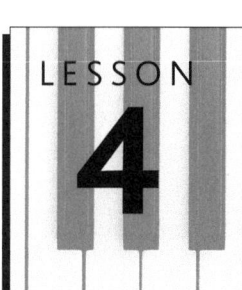

LESSON 4

NO, THIS DOESN'T MEAN chopping it in half! Go to your **auto-accompaniment** control and change the setting from **normal** to **single-finger chords***.

Your keyboard has now been divided electronically into two distinct sections: a MELODY section and an ACCOMPANIMENT section:

* Your owner's manual will tell you how to select single-finger chords on your particular instrument.

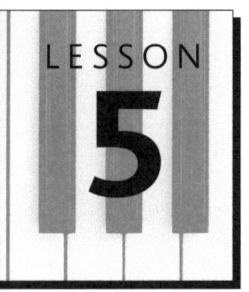

Lesson 5

Accompaniment Section

YOUR **ACCOMPANIMENT** SECTION is situated at the bottom end (left hand side) of your keyboard. It will probably have note names (letters) displayed above or below it:

accompaniment section

Accompaniment sections usually run from C to F. Check that you have **single-finger chords** selected, then play any note in your accompaniment section with finger 2 of your left hand.
You are now hearing a **chord** (three notes playing together).

Play a few more single notes at random in your accompaniment section and listen to the chords which your keyboard is playing automatically for you. (NB: You may have to activate your **style** or **rhythm** section to make these single-finger chords work. If so, select any rhythm, say **rock** and press start.)

C and G Chords

Now let's learn two specific chords.
Do you remember how the note C looks, in relation to its two adjacent black keys?

accompaniment section

* accompaniment sections do vary. On some models the accompaniment section range is from C to G; on some models the 'single-finger chord' range is only from C to C. See your owner's manual for more information.

Check that you still have **single-finger chords** set on your keyboard, then play the *higher* of the two C's with your left hand 2nd finger: C

Left Hand

You are now playing the chord of **C**, which is written in a box, like this: C

You can check that you are playing C if your keyboard has letter names printed above the accompaniment section.

Do you remember how **G** looks, in relation to its three neighbouring black keys? Play the LOWER of the two G's with your left hand 5th finger: G

Left Hand

Check your G against the letters on the keyboard.

You are now playing a chord of G, which is written like this: G

11

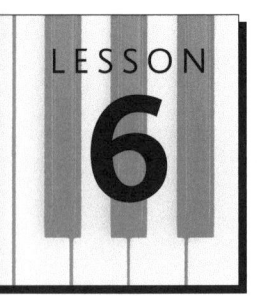

Adding Rhythm To Your Chords

IN THE STYLE (RHYTHM) section of your keyboard, select rock pop (or a similar style) and press the SYNCHRO-START button (nothing will happen for the moment).

In your AUTO-ACCOMPANIMENT section, select **single-finger chords**:

Play C (left hand finger 2) and your rhythm section will start up on a chord of **C**.

Now change to G (left hand finger 5) and listen to a chord of **G**.

Alternate between the two chords a few times.
For variation, change the rhythm from **rock pop** to **bossa nova**:

Beats And Bars

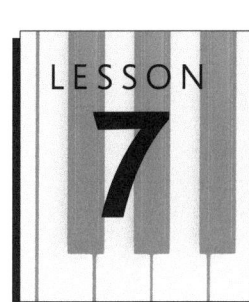

LESSON 7

WHEN YOU WERE PLAYING, did you feel the natural pulse of the music? Underlying most popular music there are pulses, or **beats**, which have a regularly recurring accent:

beats: **1** 2 3 4 **1** 2 3 4 **1** 2 3 4 (etc.)
         >   >   >

When writing this down, vertical lines, called **bar lines**, are placed in front of the first (accented) beat:

beats: |**1** 2 3 4 |**1** 2 3 4 |**1** 2 3 4 | (etc.)
       ↑   ↑   ↑   ↑
bar lines

As well as denoting the natural accents of the piece, these bar lines divide the music up into **bars**, or **measures**:

        bar (measure) 1   **bar 2**   **bar 3**
beats: |**1** 2 3 4 |**1** 2 3 4 |**1** 2 3 4 | (etc.)

Playing On The Beat

The following song accompaniment will give you practice in counting beats.

Set up your keyboard as shown at the beginning of the piece, then press **start**.
Listen to the rhythm for a while, then try counting a regular "**1**, **2**, **3**, **4**" to it.
When it sounds right to you, play a chord of C (left hand finger 2), and start following the written music.

After two bars of C, change to a chord of G (left hand finger 5).
Play right through the piece like this, following the music carefully.

White Rose Of Athens – Accompaniment

Style (or rhythm): **8 beat light**
Tempo: **medium** (♩=116)
Single-finger chords: **on**

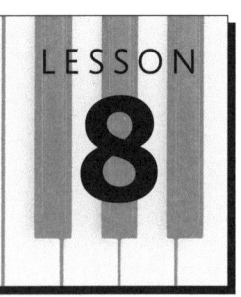

Melody Section

AS YOU LEARNT EARLIER, when you select **single-finger chords** on your keyboard the keyboard splits electronically into two sections:

The **melody** section usually begins at G, but check with your manual for any differences.

In the **melody** section you play the tune (melody) of the piece, with your right hand. The **voices** (piano, flute, violin etc) apply only to the **melody** section since, when the keyboard is split, the **accompaniment** section has its own fixed sound.

White Rose Of Athens – Melody Only

To play the melody of 'White Rose Of Athens' you need the following five notes, which you play with your right hand:

MIDDLE C (Generally the C closest to the middle of your keyboard)

Right Hand

Here are those five melody notes written down:

TREBLE CLEF (used for right hand notes)

STAVE (5 horizontal lines)

The **stave** is a sort of musical 'ladder' upon which the notes are placed. Notes can be placed **on** lines, or in the spaces **between** them. **Middle C** is too low for the stave, so a small temporary line is provided for it below the stave. These little lines (drawn above or below the stave as required) are called **ledger lines**.

White Rose Of Athens – Melody

Voice: **guitar**
Style: **8 beat light**
Tempo: **medium** (♩= 116)

1. Start with your right thumb (finger 1) on **middle C**, and play the middle C note six times in all, as written.

2. Move up step by step, through D and E, and back to D again. The D note plays eight times in all.

3. Reach up and play G three times with your fifth finger, then move down step by step, through F and E (E plays twice), then back to D (D plays twice).

Follow the song carefully through like this, noting especially when the notes repeat or move by step.

Note Values

IN THE PREVIOUS 'simplified' version of 'White Rose Of Athens' all the notes were the same length and followed the beat exactly. These 'beat' notes, called **quarter notes** or **crotchets**, are written like this:

TIME SIGNATURE
Indicates 4 "quarter notes" (crotchets) per bar

Of course tunes do not slavishly follow the beat like this as a rule. Rather they employ a mixture of **long** and **short** notes:

Note Values

♩ or ♩	**quarter note (crotchet)**	1 beat
♩ or ♩	**half note (minim)**	hold for 2 beats
♩. or ♩.	**dotted half note (dotted minim)**	hold for 3 beats
o	**whole note (semibreve)**	hold for 4 beats

In the final (correct) version of 'White Rose Of Athens' (facing page), some of the melody notes fall on the beat, others must be held longer:

Ties

Any note can be made to last longer by means of a **tie**:

Work through the whole of 'White Rose Of Athens' now, right hand only, counting the beats and playing and holding down the notes correctly, as indicated by the music. When you have mastered the right hand try adding the left hand chords.

White Rose Of Athens

Original Words & Music by Manos Hadjidakis & Hans Bradtke | English Words by Norman Newell | Additional Words by Archie Bleyer

Voice: **mandolin (or folk guitar)**
Style: **(Rhythm) 8 beat light**
Tempo: **medium (♩= 116)**

© Copyright 1961 Kassner & Company Musikverlag, Germany.
Edward Kassner Music Company Limited.
All Rights Reserved. International Copyright Secured.

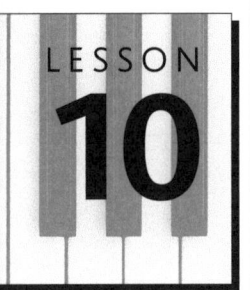

Fingered Chords

UP TO NOW you have been using a 'single-finger' chord system in your left hand. You can stay with single-finger chords for the rest of this course and beyond, if you wish, but if you want to develop your musical potential to the full you should think of changing to real chords – in other words, **fingered chords**, now:

Here are your first two fingered chords:

Play the two chords separately at first, to get the feel of them, then try moving from one to the other.
Since the bottom note **G** is common to both chords, it is good practice to hold it down during the changes.

Fingered Chord Exercise 1

Style (Rhythm): **Rock**
Tempo: **Medium** (♩ = 112)
Fingered chords: **On**

Repeat sign
go back to the opposite facing sign and repeat

New Chord: F

Single-finger chord method:
SINGLE-FINGER CHORDS ON

Fingered chord method:
FINGERED CHORDS ON

Left Hand   Left Hand

Fingered Chord Exercise 2

Fingered chords: **On**
Rhythm: **Rock**
Tempo: **Medium**

Hold down middle note (**C**) throughout (optional)

Fingered Chord Exercise 3

Fingered chords: **On**
Rhythm: **Rock**
Tempo: **Medium**

count: 4/4 ‖: F 1 2 3 4 | G 1 2 3 4 | 1 2 3 4 | C 1 2 3 4 :‖

Playing Legato

LEGATO is an Italian word, meaning *smooth, joined-up*. As you play through the melodies of the next two songs, walk very precisely from finger to finger, releasing the old finger exactly as the new finger goes down. There should be no breaks in sound between the notes, nor ugly overlaps. This joined-up style of playing is called legato. **You always play legato, unless the music is marked otherwise.**

Bye Bye Love

Words & Music by Felice & Boudleaux Bryant

The Everly Brothers

Voice: **Vibraphone**
Style: **Swing**
Tempo: **Fairly fast** (♩=132)

Bye,   Bye   love.   Bye,   Bye,
count: 1 2 3 4   1 2 3 4   1 2 3 4

hap - pi - ness.   Hel - lo   lone - li - ness, I
1 2 3 4   1 2 3 4   1 2 3 4

think I'm gon - na cry.   Bye, bye, love.
1 2 3 4   1 2 3 4   1 2 3 4   1 2 3 4

Bye, bye, sweet ca - ress.   Hel - lo   emp - ti - ness, I
1 2 3 4   1 2 3 4   1 2 3 4   1 2 3 4

feel like I could die.   Bye, bye, my love, bye, bye.
1 2 3 4   1 2 3 4   1 2 3 4   1 2 3 4

© Copyright 1957 House Of Bryant Publications, USA. Acuff-Rose Music Limited.
All Rights Reserved. International Copyright Secured.

Bad Moon Rising

Words & Music by John C. Fogerty

Creedence Clearwater Revival

Voice: **Distorted Guitar**
Style: **8 Beat Pop**
Tempo: **Medium** (♩=150)

© Copyright 1969 Jondora Music, USA.
Burlington Music Company Limited.
All Rights Reserved. International Copyright Secured.

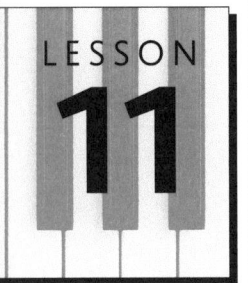

Pick-Up Notes

SONGS DO NOT ALWAYS begin on beat 1. In your next song, 'One More Night' by Phil Collins, the melody actually begins on beat 2:

One More Night (excerpt)

The three preliminary notes at the beginning of 'One More Night' are called pick-up notes.

Beats missing from the pick-up bar appear (usually) in the last bar of the song:

One More Night (excerpt)

Arranging things in this way means that you can go around the song again if you wish, keeping the beats intact.

NOTE: It is usual to play *no chord* (written N.C.) during pick-up notes.

Synchro (Synchro-Start)

IT IS WITH SONGS beginning with pick-up notes that the SYNCHRO-START feature becomes useful.

When you activate your **synchro** button your rhythm section does not begin until you play the first left hand chord. This makes a neat beginning to the song.

One More Night

Words & Music by Phil Collins

Phil Collins

Voice: **alto saxophone**
Style: **16 beat ballad**
Tempo: **medium** (♩=92)
Synchro-start: **on**

© Copyright 1984 Philip Collins Limited/Hit & Run Music (Publishing) Limited.
All Rights Reserved. International Copyright Secured.

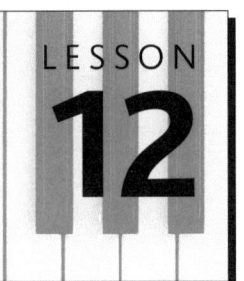

Three New Notes: A, B, C

For Right Hand

Fingering The New Notes

Now that you are moving beyond the original playing range of your five fingers, new fingering techniques will have to be adopted if the music is to remain legato.

Rio Grande (excerpt)

Don't jump here – stretch out for the high C.

Mr Tambourine Man (excerpt)

In **bar 3**, stretch out a little to play the E.

In **bar 4**, squeeze together a little to pick up the new hand position, then stretch out to play E and C.

Remember: as soon as you have completed any stretching movements in a song, let your hand return to its normal, relaxed five finger playing position (see page 5).

Rests

SILENCES ARE OFTEN called for in music. In order to indicate these, symbols called **rests** are used. Each note value has its own rest:

Rests are used mainly for musical or dramatic reasons. However, they are also useful for moving your hand from one part of the keyboard to another:

Rio Grande (excerpt)

Quarter (crotchet) rest.
(Use the break to move your hand to its new position.)

Waltz Time

SO FAR ALL OUR SONGS have been in four-four time (4/4).

However, many popular songs have **three** beats to the bar, rather than four. Songs in 3/4 time (3 quarter notes per bar) are called **Waltzes**. Our next song, 'Rio Grande', is a waltz.

Rio Grande

Traditional

Voice: **harmonica**
Style: **country waltz**
Tempo: **medium** (♩ = 100)
Synchro-start: **on**

VERSES*

CHORUS**

© Copyright 2003 Dorsey Brothers Music Limited.
All Rights Reserved. International Copyright Secured.

Continuing verses:

Verse 2
Oh, New York City is no place for me, away, Rio
I'll pack my bags and then I'll go out to sea
And we're bound for the Rio Grande
And away, Rio (etc.)

Verse 3
The anchor's aweigh and the sails they are set, away, Rio
The girls we are leaving we'll never forget
And we're bound for the Rio Grande
And away, Rio (etc.)

Verse 4
So pack up your sea bag and get underway, away, Rio
Perhaps we'll return again another day
And we're bound for the Rio Grande
And away, Rio (etc.)

Verse 5
A jolly good mate and a jolly good crew, away, Rio
A jolly good ship and a good skipper too
And we're bound for the Rio Grande
And away, Rio (etc.)

Verse 6
Now you lovely ladies, we would let you know, away, Rio
That the time has come, and we're about to go
And we're bound for the Rio Grande
And away, Rio (etc.)

Verse 7
Sing goodbye to Sally, and goodbye to Sue, away, Rio
And to all you listening, it's goodbye too
And we're bound for the Rio Grande
And away, Rio (etc.)

Blowin' In The Wind

Words & Music by Bob Dylan

Bob Dylan

Voice: **oboe**
Style: **8 beat ballad**
Tempo: **medium** (♩ = 104)

© Copyright 1962 M. Witmark & Sons, USA.
© Copyright renewed 1990 Special Rider Music, USA.
All Rights Reserved. International Copyright Secured.

Mr. Tambourine Man

Words & Music by Bob Dylan

Bob Dylan

Voice: **12 string guitar**
Style: **8 beat light**
Tempo: **medium** (♩ = 116)
Synchro-start: **on**

30

© Copyright 1964 M. Witmark & Sons, USA.
© Copyright renewed 1992 Special Rider Music, USA.
All Rights Reserved. International Copyright Secured.

31

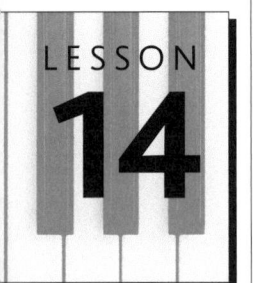

New Right Hand Notes: D, E, F, G

Where Have All The Flowers Gone?

Words & Music by Pete Seeger

Pete Seeger

Voice: **flute**
Style: **8 beat ballad**
Tempo: **medium** (♩= 100)

VERSES

Where have all the flow - ers gone, long time
1 2 3 4 1 2 3 4 1 2 3 4

pass - ing? Where have all the flow - ers gone,
1 2 3 4 1 2 3 4 1 2 3 4

long time a - go? Where have all the
1 2 3 4 1 2 3 4 1 2 3 4

flow - ers gone? Young girls picked them ev - 'ry one.
1 2 3 4 1 2 3 4 1 2 3 4

© Copyright 1961 Sanga Music Incorporated, USA.
Harmony Music Limited.
All Rights Reserved. International Copyright Secured.

Eighth Notes (Quavers)

The eighth note, or **quaver**, is a new note value:

Eighth notes move twice as fast as quarter notes:

In other words, if a quarter note is worth one beat, an eighth note is worth half a beat. If you say the word 'and' in between the beat numbers you will get the feel of the eighth note:

count: 1　　2　　3　　4　　　1 and 2 and 3 and 4 and

Keep the basic beats very regular here, then fit the quaver notes *exactly* in between them.

Like all the other note values, the eighth note has its own rest:

Eighth (quaver) rest　　equivalent to　　lasting

♫　　　　　　　　　♪　　　　　　　½ beat

Count eighth rests in exactly the same way that you would count eighth notes:

Yellow (excerpt)

Look at the stars　　　look how they shine　for　you,
I came a-long,　　　I wrote a song　for　you,

count:　　1 and 2 and 3 4　　1 and 2 and 3 4　　　2 3 4

Yellow

Words & Music by Guy Berryman, Jon Buckland, Will Champion & Chris Martin

Coldplay

Voice: **piano**
Style: **8 beat light**
Tempo: **slow** (♩ = 86)

Look at the stars look how they shine for you,
I came a-long, I wrote a song for you,
count: 1 and 2 and 3 4 1 and 2 and 3 4 2 3 4

and ev-'ry-thing you do, yeah, they were all yel - low.
and all the things you do, and it was called yel - low.
1 and 2 and 3 4 1 2 3 4 1 and 2 and 3 4 1 2 3 4

Your skin,___ oh yeah, your skin and bones, turn in___
1 2 3 4 1 and 2 and 3 and 4 1 2 3 4

to some-thing beau-ti-ful. D'you know___ you know I love you so.
1 and 2 and 3 and 4 1 2 3 4 1 and 2 and 3 and 4

You know I love you so. PAUSE
1 2 3 4 1 and 2 and 3 and 4 1 2 3 4

© Copyright 2000 BMG Music Publishing Limited.
All Rights Reserved. International Copyright Secured.

35

Imagine

Words & Music by John Lennon

John Lennon

Voice: **piano**
Style: **slow ballad**
Tempo: **slow** (♩ = 80)

I - ma-gine there's no hea - ven, it's ea - sy if you

count: 1 and 2 and 3   4   1   2   3   4   1 and 2 and 3   4

try.   No hell be - low us,

1   2   3   4   1   2 and 3   4   1   2   3   4

a - bove us on - ly sky.   I - ma-gine all the

1   2 and 3 and 4 and   1   2   3   4   1 and 2 and 3   4

peo - ple   liv - ing for to - day.   A - ha.

1 and 2   3   4   1   2   3   4   1   2   3 and 4 and

I - ma-gine there's no coun - tries, it is - n't hard to

1 and 2 and 3   4   1   2   3   4   1 and 2 and 3   4

© 1971 Lenono Music.
All Rights Reserved. International Copyright Secured.

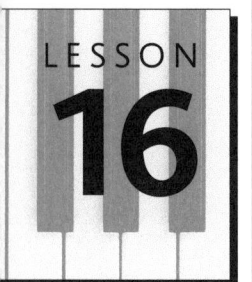

Legato And Staccato

AS YOU KNOW, **legato** means joined up or connected. When you play legato you move smoothly from finger to finger, leaving no gaps between notes. Notes which are to be played legato are often indicated on the music by a curved line called a **slur** or **phrase mark**:

Do Wah Diddy Diddy (excerpt)

When there are no slurs or other markings to the contrary, play legato.

When a single note amongst a group of staccato notes is to be played legato, it is sometimes marked like this, and called **tenuto**:

Seasons In The Sun (excerpt)

The opposite of legato is **staccato**, which means 'cut short'.

To play staccato, release the note as soon as it has been played, using a sort of 'pecking' movement of the hand. Notes which are to be played staccato are indicated on the music by dots above or below the note:

Do Wah Diddy Diddy (excerpt)

Do Wah Diddy Diddy

Words & Music by Jeff Barry & Ellie Greenwich

Manfred Mann

Voice: **trumpet**
Style: **8-beat up-tempo**
Tempo: **medium** ($\quarternote = 120$)
Synchro-start: **on**

1. There she was, just a - walk - in' down the street, } sing - in'
   we're to - ge - ther near - ly ev - 'ry sin - gle day, }
count: 1   2 and 3   4 and   1 and 2 and 3   4 and

"Do wah did - dy, did - dy dum did - dy do."
 1   2 and 3 and 4 and 1   2 and 3

Snap - pin' her fin - gers and   shuf - fl - in' her feet, } sing - in'
We're so hap - py and that's   how we're gon - na stay, }
 1 and 2 and 3 and 4   1   2 and 3   4 and

"Do wah did - dy, did-dy dum did-dy do." Looked good, (looked good). Looked
 1   2 and 3 and 4 and   1   2 and 3   4   1   2   3   4

fine (looked fine). Looked good, looked fine and I near-ly lost my mind. 2. Now.
 1   2   3   4   1   2   3   4 and   1 and 2 and 3   4

© Copyright 1964 Trio Music Company Incorporated, USA
Carlin Music Corporation.
All Rights Reserved. International Copyright Secured.

Seasons In The Sun

Words by Rod McKuen | Music by Jacques Brel

Westlife

Voice: **accordion**
Style: **slow rock**
Tempo: **medium** (♩ = 88)

VERSES

Good - bye to you, my trust - ed friend,
count: 1 and 2 and 3 and 4 and 1 2 3 4

we've known each other since we were nine___ or ten.___
1 and 2 and 3 and 4 and 1 and 2 and 3 4

To - ge - ther we've climbed hills and trees, learned of love and A B
1 and 2 and 3 and 4 and 1 2 3 4 1 2 and 3 and 4 and

C's, skimmed our hearts, and skinned our knees. Good-bye my friend it's hard to
1 and 2 and 3 and 4 and 1 and 2 and 3 and 4 and

die, when all the birds are sing - ing in___ the sky.___
1 2 3 4 1 and 2 and 3 and 4 and 1 and 2 and 3 4

© Copyright 1961 Edward B. Marks Music Company, USA.
Carlin Music Corporation.
All Rights Reserved. International Copyright Secured.

41

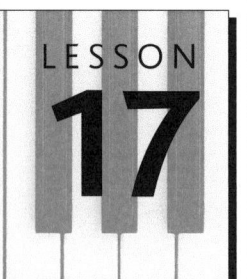

Seventh Chords

The three chords you have learnt so far: **C**, **G** and **F**, are all **major** chords. **Seventh** chords are *variations* of these chords. When using the single-finger chord method there are various ways of forming sevenths. Your owner's manual will tell you exactly how to form sevenths on your particular instrument, but the first two diagrams below show two possibilities:

Chord Of G7

Single-finger chord method

Play G, together with any white note to its LEFT.

Play G, together with any two notes to its RIGHT.

Fingered chord method

Chord Of D7

Single-finger chord method

Play D, together with any white note to its LEFT.

Play D, together with any two notes to its RIGHT.

Fingered chord method

*This symbol ♯ is called a **sharp**. It will be explained properly in Book 2, but for now simply play the black note indicated.

D.S. Al Coda And D.C. Al Coda

WE USE THESE instructions (also known as form notation) to simplify and shorten pieces of music with many repeats. Here are the main terms, and what they mean. Look out for them in the next two pieces.

DAL SEGNO (D.S.) means repeat from the sign 𝄋
FINE is the end of the piece
DAL SEGNO AL FINE (D.S. al FINE) means go back to the sign 𝄋 and play through the piece again until you reach the word FINE. This is where the piece ends.
DA CAPO means the beginning
DA CAPO (D.C.) means 'repeat from the beginning'
DA CAPO AL FINE (D.C. al FINE) means go back to the beginning of the piece and play through again until you reach the word FINE. This is where the piece ends.

Stephen Gately

Any Dream Will Do

Music by Andrew Lloyd Webber | Lyrics by Tim Rice

Voice: **string ensemble**
Style: **swing**
Tempo: **medium** (♩ = 125)
Synchro-start: **on**

© Copyright 1969 The Really Useful Group Limited.
This arrangement © Copyright 2003 The Really Useful Group Limited.
All Rights Reserved. International Copyright Secured.

Can You Feel The Love Tonight

(from Walt Disney Pictures' "The Lion King") Music by Elton John | Words by Tim Rice

Elton John

Voice: **piano**
Style: **16 beat ballad**
Tempo: **slow** (♩ = 72)

VERSES

1. There's a calm sur - ren - der to the rush of day,
2. There's a time for ev - 'ry - one if they on - ly learn

count: 1 and 2 and 3 and 4 1 and 2 and 3 4

when the heat of the roll - ing world can be turned a - way.
that the twisting ka - lai - do - scope moves us all in turn.

1 and 2 and 3 and 4 1 and 2 and 3 3

An en - chant - ed mo - ment, and it see me through,
There's a rhyme and rea - son, to the wild out - doors,

1 and 2 and 3 and 4 1 and 2 and 3 4

it's e - nough for this rest - less war - rior just to be with you. And
when the heart of this star-crossed voy - ger beats in time with yours.

1 and 2 and 3 and 4 and 1 and 2 and 3 4 and

CHORUS

can you feel the love to - night? It is where we are.

1 2 3 4 1 2 and 3 4 1 2 and 3 4 and

© Copyright 1994 Wonderland Music Company Incorporated, USA.
This arrangement © Copyright 2002 Wonderland Music Company Incorporated.
Used with permission by Music Sales Limited.
All Rights Reserved. International Copyright Secured.

Let It Be

Words & Music by John Lennon & Paul McCartney

Paul McCartney

Voice: **folk guitar**
Style: **light pop**
Tempo: **slow** (♩ = 66)
Synchro-start: **on**

VERSES

1. When I find my-self in times of trou-ble, Mo-ther Ma-ry comes to me,
all the bro-ken heart-ed peo-ple liv-ing in the world a-gree,

count: (1 2 3) 4 and   1 and 2 and 3 and 4 and   1 and 2 and 3 and 4

speak-ing words of wis-dom, let it be. And in my hour of dark-ness she is
there will be an ans-wer, let it be. For though they may be part-ed, there is

1 and 2 and 3 and 4 and   1 and 2 3 4 and   1 and 2 and 3 and 4 and

stand-ing right in front of me, speak-ing words of wis-dom, let it
still a chance that they will see, there will be an ans-wer, let it

1 and 2 and 3 and 4   1 and 2 and 3 and 4 and

be. ⎫
be. ⎭   Let it be, let it be, let it be, let it be.

1 and 2   3   4 and   1   2 and 3 and 4 and   1 and 2 and 3 and 4

Whis-per words of wis-dom, let it be._____   2. And when

1 and 2 and 3 and 4 and   1 and 2   3   4 and

© Copyright 1970 Northern Songs.
All Rights Reserved. International Copyright Secured.

* Use your volume pedal, if you have one. If not, ease back your Master Volume control bit by bit with your left hand in between playing chords.

Congratulations

... on completing Book 1 of The Complete Keyboard Player!

In Book 2 you will...

- Learn about sharps and flats
- Move to a new stage in note reading
- Increase the range of your melody playing
- Learn new left hand chords, including minor chords
- Add to your repertoire of great popular songs!